# DRAGONS' DEN

# DRAGONS' DEN

# YOUR ROAD TO SUCCESS

**BBC LARGE PRINT**

First published in 2009 by
HarperCollins Publishers
This Large Print edition published
2009 by BBC Audiobooks by
arrangement with
HarperCollins Publishers Ltd

ISBN 978 1 405 62257 8

All other text supplied by Premium Publishing
By arrangement with the BBC and Sony
Pictures Television International

Quick Reads™ used under licence.

British Library Cataloguing in Publication Data available

Printed and bound in Great Britain by
CPI Antony Rowe, Chippenham and Eastbourne

## About the authors

Deborah Meaden began her own glass and ceramics export company as soon as she had finished business college. Duncan Bannatyne started his business career with an ice-cream van he bought for £450. Peter Jones was only 16 when he started his first tennis academy. Theo Paphitis has made a success of many failing businesses, and James Caan is an experienced investor and a multi-millionaire.

# Contents

Introduction • 1

Chapter 1—Peter Jones • 3

Chapter 2—Deborah Meaden • 21

Chapter 3—Theo Paphitis • 41

Chapter 4—Duncan Bannatyne • 59

Chapter 5—James Caan • 78

# Introduction

What makes a Dragon? They all have one thing in common. They have lots of money, and they made it themselves. So, are the rich different to us? Well actually no. Their lives are very similar to ours but with a few key differences. You are about to meet five very successful people.

Theo came to the UK from Cyprus, and was already involved in business by the time he was twenty.

Duncan had an ice-cream van and liked to tell people what he really thought of them. He didn't start running businesses until much later, but his understanding of people is the skill that has made him millions.

Deborah began her career when she was seven years old, running a little flower stall outside her house. She now uses her sales and marketing skills to help the businesses she has invested in.

Peter is very competitive. He's had this quality since childhood, always wanting to be top of the class and to win at tennis. He still wants to win even now, and he uses his natural talent to be the best in his field.

James is a gentleman, who is good with people, and this skill has been vital to his success.

All our Dragons have their feet on the ground and live in the real world. Their stories can tell us a great deal about what it takes to become successful.

# Peter Jones

## The Creative Thinker

Peter Jones was born in 1966 and raised in Berkshire. He attended state schools, apart from a short time at a private school when he was seven. Peter set up his own tennis school at sixteen and his second business when he was only eighteen. In his twenties he ran a thriving computer company but difficulties caused him to lose that business.

At the age of twenty-eight Peter joined a large company and ran its computer business in the United Kingdom. In 1998 he founded a phone company that now makes more than $250 million a year. His businesses include a range of companies in lots of different areas.

Peter has won many awards and is committed to helping young people start their own businesses. Peter works closely with the government, helping to make Britain more successful. Peter's story shows just how much drive you need to succeed. Peter's need to win, and his desire not to give up, are the skills that have made him so successful.

*      *      *

I've always been someone who does what they want to do. I've been able to make my own choices from an early age. My parents sent me to a smart private school for a short time because they wanted the best for me. However, it was a lot stricter than state school and much more was expected of me. I struggled in class, so I spent a lot of time working very hard to keep up. I wanted to be top of the class, but I knew that I couldn't be because there were some very clever boys there. Even at that early age I knew that the way to be successful was through determination and hard work.

I always loved sport at school though, especially tennis. I never liked being second-best, so when I was playing tennis, I was competitive. If I lost points or games, I'd end up chucking my racket on the ground. I always thought I'd get to Wimbledon, and I wanted to be the world's best tennis player. I'd spend every spare minute hitting a ball against the house wall pretending I was at Wimbledon. My mum had to put her earplugs in. I went back to state school and then, from the age of eleven until I was eighteen, I played tennis seven days a week. I played UK competitions all over the country. Even though I knew tennis was just a game, I still really wanted to win.

Tennis is an intelligent game. In many ways tennis is similar to business. The skills I learned playing it have helped my career. In tennis you've got to work out your tactics, understand your playing partner and size up their game. It's important to have confidence from the moment you walk onto the court. There is, however, a key difference between tennis and success at work. Business is not about winning at all costs. At work you need to find ways where you both benefit. It's not like tennis where the winner takes all. I don't want to do a deal with somebody and walk out thinking, 'Ah, got them'. That's not how I work. Being successful is about teamwork and working together towards a shared goal. At work I want my colleagues to be happy, and for me to feel exactly the same. In tennis the last thing I want to do is walk off a court when somebody else has won the match. I'm out there to win. In business I want both of us to win.

However, when it comes to competitors, sport and business are very similar. After all, there are two types of tennis. When you play singles, you're on the court on your own.

There's no one to help you and no one else to blame, and it's about beating the other player. When you play doubles, there's somebody else that you've got to rely on, work with and talk to. For me, that's how successful people behave at work. Often in business you start on your own and you need to win every deal to make money. Then you get staff and you work as a team to be successful. Together you plan and work to beat the competition.

My first company built computer systems and provided computer support. It did well during the 1980s, but I lost sight of the most important part of running a company. I got carried away with my own success, thinking it was easy, without seeing the risks. I was supplying goods to customers on credit without making sure they could pay. At some point there was going to be a problem . . . and there was! Lots of companies that I was supplying went bust owing me many thousands of pounds and my business collapsed.

For a while, I hoped to save my company. I think it took me twenty-four hours to realise that I couldn't. I was twenty-nine and I had lost everything. I had nowhere to live, so I moved into the office building where I started and thought about how I could start again. I didn't have any money or a car but I wasn't sitting around weeping. I was thinking, 'Well, I've got myself into this, so I'm going to get out of it. It's as simple as that. I've lost my BMW, my Porsche and my house. I've lost everything. Well, it's not the end of the world.' Very few people have a smooth ride getting to the top. Often the most successful people are those who have lost a job or a business, and have learned from their mistakes.

The main lesson from the collapse of my company was that I had got too carried away with making sales and had not looked at the bigger picture.

Once I'd learned that lesson I never made the same mistake again. After that I always made sure that I had insurance to protect my business. Even successful people make mistakes. That's how we learn. The important thing is to pick yourself up and not make the same mistakes again.

In 1998 I started a telephone company. It was clear to me that everybody was soon going to be walking around with a mobile phone. I worked with a factory and bought a large number of phones to supply to smaller businesses who couldn't afford to buy them in large numbers. I knew mobile phones would make me wealthy, but I had no idea they would make me tens of millions.

There were a lot of similar businesses starting then, but what we did was different. Nobody else had decided to supply just one type of phone and build a name based on one product. So I formed a good relationship with the makers of the phone and we became the only company to supply that phone. That way we could buy a lot more phones, which meant we could both buy and sell them more cheaply.

As a result, we became one of the fastest growing businesses in Europe. Was I lucky? I don't think so. I saw an opportunity, made a plan, and worked very hard. That made me successful. Having a clear idea of what you want to achieve and believing in yourself are some of the most important assets in life.

In the first three or four months there were only a couple of us, and then we started to hire people. Getting the right people wasn't easy because at that stage we were just a small company. We wanted local people, so we looked around and talked to people with energy and drive. I always knew having good people was going to be key to our success. Good people doesn't just mean efficient people. It means people who have a great attitude and who will put everything they've got into the company. Finding and working with great people has always been, and still is, a big part of my success.

After a few years we had offices in England, France and Romania. Now we're not just involved in mobile phones. We deal with computers and the internet and we work with some of the world's biggest companies.

I now work on many projects including finance, property and TV. I'm always looking for new projects, and I have a team of people who look at people's ideas and give them feedback. Perhaps a few will get a phone call to say that we would like to see them and talk about their idea. I get very excited about this work. Some people have held business ideas for a long time but have never told anyone. This is their chance to be able to say, 'Peter Jones thinks this is a good idea' or 'Peter Jones thinks it's a really bad idea and that I should drop it. Well, at least I've had a go.'

My advice is to always have a plan. Whether you are going for a job interview or starting your first company, have a clear idea of what you want and what you can offer. Getting ahead is easier when you can see what you want to achieve. Then, be prepared to work hard to achieve your goals. And lastly, if you make a mistake, learn from it and then pick yourself up and carry on.

Here are some of my tips for success:

## 1. Enjoy your work

First of all, you need to enjoy what it is that you do. If you are not excited by your work, you won't do a great job. Being excited by what you do doesn't mean you have to love your job all the time, but you must believe that it is worthwhile. If you're studying at an evening class, you should get a sense of achievement from it. So, don't work on a business project if you can't get excited by the idea. Ask the questions: Do I really care? Does it make a difference to me?

Personally, I'm not interested in putting money into a business and just letting it go. I am not a gambler. I don't throw my money around. When I'm in the Dragons' Den I ask myself 'Does it grab me?' Then, finally, 'Can Peter Jones make a difference?' Because, if I can't offer something new to a project I am involved with, what's the point?

## 2. Think about it

Think carefully about whether your goals are really possible. Think everything through. This is my key piece of advice: do your research. Whether you are going for a job or college interview or starting a company, research is vital. When you go for an interview make sure you know about the company and be ready to answer questions.

In business, some projects that sound good will quickly reveal problems. Make sure your plan is based on solid research. Think about the questions that you might need to answer and plan ahead for them. If you're thinking of starting your own company, be realistic about the amount of capital and cash that a company needs. It may well be more than you think. Also, be realistic about the potential of the company and its sales. Proper funding is critical to success.

If you're applying to college, think about how you are going to fund the course and your studying time. Look into what money is available and start thinking about your budget. In other words, dream big, but do your homework. You need to know that you can turn dreams into reality. This takes research, groundwork and realistic figures.

## 3. Look out for big ideas

Work out the upside, how big an idea is. Ask the question: how successful could this be? I like to know how big the market for the product or service could be. Is it international? When I know the scale, I can then assess how much profit it could deliver and how much money I could make.

For example, being on television opened my eyes to a very big opportunity. I realised that over the next twenty years television and media will be web-based, and that more people will use the internet and broadband to view television programmes on demand. Of course now I have moved into that area of business.

## 4. Be passionate and persistent

Once I have invested in a business, or started it, I'm passionate about making it work. You need to keep that passion to help you commit to getting things done. It will also strengthen the inner belief you need to succeed. If you *believe* that you will succeed, you are far more likely to do so. Passion will drive you forward when things get tough and give you extra persistence. My 'keep on keeping on' policy comes from my passion for what I do. Don't give up when you come across the first problem. Work out a way around it, learn from it and then carry on.

## 5. Develop your instinct

I am not academic. I struggled at school. But that doesn't matter. To succeed in business you need a nose for a good opportunity. Often you have to let your gut feeling guide you. Instinct can be more important than passing exams and the skill is to see the potential in something that, at first, doesn't look promising.

Economists are sometimes surprised by our investments because they are used to theories and figures. When those don't add up, they can't see the potential. Although theories and figures are important in business, thinking beyond them is an essential skill. I can look at an idea that might not seem to have any worth and find a way to make it work. When Peter Ashley came to us with an exercise chair that fell apart, it seemed a ridiculous idea. But, if he had re-built it as a fitness chair for people with health problems, perhaps he could have got the Dragons interested. My instinct told me his idea had potential. It just needed a re-think.

## 6. Presentation is all-important

How you look, how you speak, and how clearly you can explain your product or service all contribute to how seriously you will be taken. Presentation doesn't have to follow any rules, but it does need to be carefully thought through. As soon as Levi Roots was halfway up the stairs on *Dragons' Den*, his singing made me smile. I didn't have a clue about the product, but because he was fun and engaging, I couldn't wait to find out what it was. It was a unique, compelling start to a pitch. His sauce has achieved cult status in this country, outselling tomato ketchup. Levi's is an amazing success story.

## 7. Know what you want to achieve and focus on results

Imran Hakim is a good example of a businessman who knows what he wants to achieve. He saw that 'kids are getting older, younger,' and that they want the same kind of technology their older brothers and sisters have. So Imran came up with the idea of a soft toy with a screen in its belly. He believed that his iTeddy would be the next bestselling toy at Christmas. He gave us figures that he thought he could achieve, told us who he thought he could sell it to, and who would buy it. He told us why people would want it. He gave us an example of why iTeddy would be successful, because it would be based around cartoon or bedtime stories downloaded directly to the teddy. People would come back to buy more. For me, it was a great idea and I couldn't wait to do the deal. I liked the amount of energy Imran had put into understanding his product and what he wanted to achieve.

## 8. Timing is all-important
Starting any project will demand your complete commitment. Things can be difficult when you start a new job or a new business project, and there are times in life when it might not be best to take on that commitment. An understanding partner, good health and the right circumstances are important for success. Get your timing right, and remember that everyone needs others to help them, even the most successful people. Look out for people who will provide the right support at the right time.

## 9. You need drive and confidence to succeed

You'll know this if you play a sport. In many ways, tennis is similar to business, and the skills I learned on court have helped my business career. In tennis you've got to come up with a plan, understand your tennis partner, and then assess your competitor, sizing up their game. In the Dragons' Den my strategy is not to ask too many questions at first, because then I'm giving information to the other Dragons. I wait for them to say whether they are out first. Then I ask the questions that could give me the answers to make me really want to invest.

Finally, whether you're walking onto a tennis court or entering a business setting, there are two things to remember: have confidence in yourself, and never give up.

# Deborah Meaden

## The Marketing Expert

Deborah Meaden joined Dragons' Den for the third series and is the only female Dragon. She was born in 1959 and set up her first company selling glass and ceramics from Italy shortly after she left college. She worked in fashion and at Butlins before joining her family's amusement arcade business.

After working her way to the top, she founded Weststar Holidays with her parents. She was made Managing Director and grew the company into a business providing high-quality family holidays for over 100,000 people every year. Deborah sold the company in a deal worth £33 million.

Deborah now spends half her time in London and half in the south of England in the home she shares with her husband, Friday the cat, two dogs, five horses, eleven chickens and four ducks. Deborah has always understood her customers and goes out of her way to find out what they want. This customer care and attention to detail has given her the edge when it comes to business.

*    *    *

I was always going to run my own business. It never entered my head that I was ever going to work for anyone else. When I was seven years old I set up a flower stall at our gate, stocked with flowers I'd picked from our garden. I soon realised that the location was wrong because everybody was driving the wrong way. So I then moved my stall to our neighbour's gate—much to her disgust! Finding the right location was a vital lesson when it came to holiday parks, so I'm glad I learned it early.
I am a very confident person and I

think that confidence is the key to success. People buy from confident people.

When I left school, I wanted to be in London, but I had no reason to be there or money to afford it. So I answered an advert for a model in the sales room of a London fashion house. You had to be 5 ft 8" and I'm 5 ft 1", but I thought if I could just get in the door, I could talk my way into a job. And that's what happened. Clearly they believed that my confidence and sales ability would make up for my lack of height.

I was always looking for ways to start my own business. After college I stayed with a friend in Italy. I noticed some wonderful glass and ceramics, and thought, 'I haven't seen this in the UK'. I had no money to buy stock but I did have sales skills. I was only nineteen and I just knocked on doors and said, 'Look, I've got no sales network but I will work my socks off to sell your goods in the UK'. People agreed. Then I got the goods into an important trade fair. From there, I started selling to some of the bigger stores, like Harvey Nichols.

I went through a series of businesses after that. The one I learned most from was a prize bingo hall at Butlins. You deal directly with the customer and if the customer doesn't like you they walk away, and you see them do it. It was also a good lesson in understanding that time is money. If you mess around and your games go too slowly, it costs you money. The quality has got to be there too. Otherwise your customer will tell you about it.

Remembering people was a key to my success. In a day I'd probably see a thousand people. I tried to recognise and remember most of them. If I couldn't, I learned to look as if I did. Recognise people and make them feel valued, and they will remember you. This is an important lesson I learned from the bingo and I have found that it is vital to success in both work and life. Bingo is very popular, and the reason people do it is because it is sociable. So you have to make it fun and create a friendly feel.

It's the same with the whole of the leisure industry, whether it is holidays, arcades, fast-food outlets, even shopping—yes, shopping is a leisure activity. The customer needs a reason to choose what you are offering rather than the place next door. It's all about environment. You need to create a place where people feel comfortable. If someone was starting a business I would say, 'Why would the customer choose you?' In the same way, at a job interview you need to know why the employers should pick you over anyone else.

My next step was to join my parents in running amusement arcades. Again, the focus was on creating a place where people felt comfortable and on giving a good service. There might be seven arcades on the seafront, so we needed to get people to choose ours. It was about the little details: carpets, comfortable seats and making things easy for the customer. The maximum you could win was something like £1.40, so it wasn't about the winning. It was about making people feel good.

Anyone who thinks that working in a family business is the easy option is wrong. You have to be tough and face some difficult issues head-on if it is going to work. My family has always been very clear that if you look after your work it will look after you. This is very important for anyone working with close friends or family. You need to focus on the work and keep away from the personal issues. This can be difficult, but as long as you keep work separate from family matters, it can be a great working relationship.

Throughout my career, I'd been building up a picture of how people wanted to spend their leisure time. When the chance came up to buy a struggling holiday park, I went for it. This was in 1988. We ended up with a group of holiday parks, providing holidays for more than 100,000 people a year.

I was confident that I knew how to improve the holiday parks and provide what people wanted. The location had to be special—I'd never buy a holiday park in a bad location. I'd learned the value of location early on in life! We built indoor swimming pools, restaurants, clubs, tennis courts and adventure play-grounds because, in this country, the weather is always going to be a problem. By building things inside we could extend the holiday season. We managed to keep one of our parks open for forty-eight weeks, which was a record. It sounds simple now, but we were one of the first holiday parks to build indoor swimming pools.

In 1999 I sold half my stake in the business in a deal worth £33 million. I still owned some of Weststar and played an active role in the bigger decisions but withdrew from the day-to-day running of the company. In 2007 I sold the remainder of my stake, at which time Weststar was valued at £83 million.

Now that I spend less time on the day-to-day running of a business, I have had more time to become involved with other projects. I like to get involved in a project right at the very beginning and enjoy really being able to make a difference. Most of all, I love success and successful people and I get a real buzz out of seeing a business I am involved in succeed.

I think my greatest strengths lie in sales, marketing and understanding people. As a result of this I have invested in a research company. I am a great believer in research and think that, whatever your line of work, it is a key to success. If you are thinking of starting a business, then you need to find out whether there are people wanting to buy that product or use that service. If you're applying for a job, find out about the company. The internet makes this easy. You can find out all the things you need to know quickly and without any hassle. The key is to make sure your research is useful. Focus and don't get distracted!

Sales and marketing are not as complex as some people make them seem. You need to think about the customer buying your product or using your service. Work out the types of people that buy your product. Then you need to think about where you could find them and how you can talk to them. It is vital to have a clear idea of your typical customer. When I invest in something I often think about this typical customer, and I want to be clear about their age, style, marital status, hobbies, leisure activities, music taste, what newspaper they would read and so on. Usually I give this fictional person a name because, even though they are not real, they represent the customer. This fictional person is a useful tool when I think about where to advertise. Would that person read this magazine? It is also a clear idea for everyone involved in the project to follow.

You must be confident to be successful, and you must always want to improve. A lot of people think that passion is enough, but it's not—and being passionate too early can be a mistake. At the start you need to be able to take a step back from the project and see if it is working. When I'm making business decisions I can be quite dispassionate. On TV my face is deadpan and, yes, there is a coolness there. I have even been called an 'Ice Queen', but that must be by somebody who hasn't seen the laughter lines. You don't get those by being cold and humourless! I have great fun at work, but I know when to be serious and I am not afraid of telling it as it is if I need to.

I've made mistakes, but I've learned from them, and I've avoided major disasters. I believe in taking risks, but not silly gambles. What would I do if I were to lose all my money? I'd make it again, of course!

When I put together my rules for success I went back to what I learned from my family. Focus on the stuff that matters. Think about who you have to sell yourself to, why they should choose you, and how to sell yourself to them. That is the way to get ahead and stay ahead.

## 1. Be honest

One of my faults is that I can be too blunt, but honesty is an asset as long as you don't go too far. I believe it is better to be straight than to waste people's valuable time and trouble. So, let me state this plainly. Whatever you do, whatever your target (to start a business, get some training, or get a job), be yourself. Give honest answers to questions, and help everyone understand your ideas and what you can offer.

Investors, employers and anyone worth knowing in life will know when someone is talking rubbish. Trying to pull the wool over their eyes is a dangerous game to play. Decent people invest in people they trust. Understanding that is your first step to success.

## 2. Do what you do best the best way you can

Some people think you have to be an accountant or a lawyer to succeed in business. That's not true. I have run holiday parks and amusement arcades, have worked in high-street fashion and have exported exclusive

Italian glass. Your success might come from anywhere. It could be engineering or garden design, or you could invent a video game or excel in sport.

One young woman I knew came up with an unusual new doll. She succeeded because she was energetic, quick-thinking and wise enough to take the right advice. Like her, you should take a cool, careful look at your ambitions and ask yourself some honest questions. How great is my talent? How hard am I prepared to work? Are there people who will support me but also help to push me as far as I can go?

Let me tell you, a lot of people want to be the best and make money from it. Few actually do it. You have to be totally sure your idea is right and that people will buy it (and you) before you go for it. Get passionate, by all means, but be one hundred per cent sure where you are going first.

## 3. Make a plan

A step-by-step plan with time scales and milestones is an excellent idea. It is like creating a map to your goals. Think where you want to go, use your knowledge and research. By all means ask other people to help you, but make sure the plan ends up yours, not theirs, so you believe in it through and through. That way, you stand a much better chance of sticking to it. If you do it to please someone else or to show off, it has no point at all.

A solid plan will give you a sense of how long things actually take. When I say I will invest in someone on Dragons' Den, they often think it will happen tomorrow. But there are all sorts of things I have to check out first. So I tell them to cut themselves some slack. Just because they wrote the plan does not mean things are going to happen exactly when they say they will. On the other hand, if you are always missing deadlines, failing to achieve targets and re-writing your plan, it means that something needs a thorough re-think.

Always keep your plan clear and simple and it will keep you on track. A stage-by-stage plan is good for your confidence when times get tough, because you can clearly see what you have already achieved.

## 4. Know your stuff

With so much information available on the internet, researching your market (or the company you've applied to for a job, or the college where you've applied to take a course) has never been easier. Make your research detailed and relevant to convince an investor or employer or college tutor that you know the important stuff.

Next comes the 'pitch' or the interview. This is where you have to tell your story. The key is to get your message across in a brief, believable way. Think carefully about what you are going to say. Don't try to be slick or too clever. If possible, rehearse in front of someone you respect and admire. Ask them for honest feedback so you can make adjustments.

Some people who pitch to us on *Dragons' Den* practise with a video camera first. Set it up at home, perform your pitch or practise your interview and then look at what you have done. It may make you blush, but it will help you see what you still need to polish. One man who came on the show told me he cringed at his first attempt. He watched it from between his fingers. It was so awful. But he saw that he had to say some things differently and explain them better. By the time he came to the Den, he was excellent. It's that kind of care and attention to detail that creates success.

## 5. Present yourself well
I have no time for people who use jargon to try to be clever. Always use

your own language. Otherwise you will baffle your audience and end up looking foolish. Before meetings, memorise your key points. Then, if you lose your thread, you can easily pick it up again. If something goes wrong, don't panic. Keep a cool head, find your place and continue.

First impressions are important too. Always make sure you look good so that you feel good. Wear your favourite suit (or suitable clothing), take time with your grooming in the morning and make sure you feel 'a million dollars'. Then stand up, keep eye contact and speak clearly. All this will help with your confidence— and confidence is catching. If you believe in yourself, then others will believe in you too.

## 6. No whingeing
To be successful at work you have to do whatever has to be done. You might have to start at the bottom and work hard before you get to do the job

you really want to do. You are responsible for your own life. When I was a child we had very little money, but my mother would never let the world get her down. I'm the same. I am not interested in self-pity. There's no point in whingeing. Move on. Nobody else is going to do it for you.

Turn mistakes to your advantage. I've made plenty of mistakes, but I learned from them and so avoided major disasters. It is better to admit that you got something wrong than to lose time and money covering it up. That is how disasters happen. Learn your lessons and keep moving forward.

## 7. One for the girls

As the only female Dragon, I get asked a lot of questions about what it's like to be a woman in a man's world. I don't see the business world like that. If someone's got a problem with me being a woman, then they had better deal with it because I'm not putting up with it.

My advice to women at work is this. First, tell whoever it is to stop being a pain. Then concentrate on your own job. For me, whatever I am involved in right now is the most important thing I could possibly be doing. Once it's over, I don't beat myself up about what I could have done differently. I just focus on the next project.

Keep your eye on the job in hand and you will soon forget about the person who was annoying you. What's more, with a bit of your own hard-earned success you have a good chance of leaving the idiot behind for ever.

# Theo Paphitis

## The Retail Expert

Theo Paphitis was born in Cyprus in 1959. His family moved to England when Theo was six years old. He went to a local school in north London where they failed to detect his dyslexia. He left to take a job as a tea-boy and filing clerk at a large London company. He made his first step into retail at the age of eighteen as a sales assistant for Watches of Switzerland.

At twenty, he moved into finance and became involved in mortgage sales. At twenty-three, he set up his own company, and later became good at turning around failing businesses. Theo has bought ailing businesses, such as the stationery chain Ryman and Partners and the La Senza and Contessa lingerie chains, and has turned them into money-making companies. He has several other business interests including a fifty per cent share in Red Letter Days, which he bought with fellow Dragon, Peter Jones.

Theo lives in Surrey with his wife Debbie. He has five children, Dominic, Zoe, Alex, Hollie and Annabelle, as well as two grandchildren. He married young and, keen to support his wife and kids, threw himself into work, picking up priceless retail tips from the shop floor. He still puts those lessons to use as a multi-millionaire business person.

\*     \*     \*

Do you ever finally 'make it' in business? I don't think so. And that's what drives me to keep going. The day I say I've 'made it' in business will be the day that I retire or die. In my case, it will probably be the former.

When I started work I was sixteen

and working in a finance company in the city as a tea-boy. No, I wasn't even that, I was the assistant to the tea stirrer! He was the official tea-boy and I just helped out. I had paired up with Mrs Paphitis by then, and I was finding it very difficult to settle down on the small salary I was earning. To be honest with you, I didn't know what I wanted at that age but I saw a job working for Watches of Switzerland advertised in the Evening Standard. It paid more than I was earning, so I went for the interview. I was offered the job on the spot and that was my first experience of the fast-paced world of retail.

I enjoyed retail from the start. I was in one of those stores where the door was always locked and people had to ring the buzzer to be let in. You never knew who was going to come in and it was exciting not knowing what would happen next. When a customer came in, you had to get to work right away.

You had to take an interest in them and work out what they wanted. You got really involved. The whole thing including, naturally, closing the sale, was right up my street.

What I want to stress here is this. The great thing about retail is that you experience advertising, you experience sales, you experience customer service and you experience design. Those are wonderful things to know about at whatever level you are. And in retail, you can learn them right at the start.

I stayed at Watches of Switzerland until I was twenty. By then, I needed more money again. As a salesman in a classy watch store you can only earn so much. I was a pretty good salesman, but the job was never going to give me enough money—and big money was my dream.

So I moved back to the finance industry, and you know what? I found I could use a lot of the skills I had. The salesman skills, the marketing skills, they had all been perfected in the years I was in retail.

Of course, I had always believed, and still preach, that business is very much about common sense. The lack of common sense out there always surprises me. Without any formal training I was meeting people and advising them on how to get their businesses back on track. It amazed me how little people knew about what they needed to do to put their businesses right.

I wonder now how I must have appeared, giving advice when I was still very young myself. Luckily, I looked a bit older than I was, and I was careful not to tell people my actual age. I was good at looking at people's companies, seeing problems, and giving advice about how to fix them. I was still using the skills that I gained from my first job in retail. What is wonderful for me is how I have been able to link my two careers and my two loves: retail and helping failing businesses.

Well, I'm one of those people who has the attention span of a gnat and, three years later, I decided to go it alone. I think this is either something you are comfortable with or something you're not. Some people like decisions to be made for them and some people like to take control. I was twenty-three when I started running my own company. I made some money in the property boom of the 1980s and kept going from there, always looking for the right deal, the right break. I learned focus and hard work.

The most important rule for me has always been to choose the right target. However tempting they may seem, some companies can never be made successful. I only look at businesses that are struggling. If a business is doing well, it is no good to me. I want a business that has got potential, that needs my input, my care, my attention to detail and my passion: for example, Movie Media Sports.

Movie Media Sports was an agency that promoted sports events. I invested forty grand in it for a fifty per cent share of the company. I had that for about ten years and made around £6 million from it. Mind you, I have to admit that it was really about having fun. I like sport and it was great to be around all the sports grounds, with passes to all the events, and to make money out of it at the same time. It doesn't get better than that, does it?

But mainly, I am drawn to brands that people recognise. A company might seem to be on its last legs, but a brand that people know can give you the edge when you come to relaunch it. I prefer the simple approach. 'Keep it Simple, Stupid' has always been my motto.

Ryman ticked all the boxes. It had been around a long time and was a household name. But when I bought it in 1995, it was in a terrible state. It had lost about £8–10 million the year before. The staff were not happy and there was no stock. We were entering the computer age and everybody was telling me that paper and pencils and pens were things of the past. But I had known Ryman as a kid, and I had actually shopped there.

I knew that I needed to plan properly and address its huge problems. Firstly, I had to get the staff onside. Without them I knew I would never succeed. I needed to get them buying into my dream, into my ambitions for the company and the brand, before I did anything else. At head office, I had to ensure people were actually doing jobs that were necessary rather than jobs for the job's sake. But the big challenge was to make the people who worked in the stores happy and excited again.

How did I do it? I did what I have done in all my businesses. I made sure that the staff had direct access to me. I would go to the stores to work with them and listen to them. This was key to the success of Ryman. Often with failed businesses one of the biggest problems is that staff feel separated from the boss. A hands-on approach is a vital part of the solution.

I worked out where we could cut costs and boost sales, and I gained back the confidence of the suppliers so that we could supply the service that our customers needed. And hey presto, the results started coming through. I had been right. Ryman was a hugely strong brand with loyal followers and, as long as we gave them the service that they wanted and had the product in the stores at the right time, customers came.

For the staff too, a sense that they could share in the success of the business made heaps of difference. All my staff are encouraged to do well. From the people in the warehouse to the drivers, from the store staff to the post lady, they are all rewarded financially when they perform well. I also like to encourage staff with conferences and social functions. I have found that these occasions are useful for getting feedback on what's going on in the stores and the business.

And, the funny thing is that all this comes from my days at Watches of Switzerland. I learned that head office never listened, so I do listen. I learned as a young salesman that, if I sold a product that had a yellow sticker on it, I got ten per cent commission. Guess what most of my sales were? So now I make sure that I always give proper incentives to my staff.

Retail is all about detail, about being sure that everything is right for the customer. At La Senza, the lingerie chain, I took pride in making our customers feel special. Their garment would be wrapped in tissue paper with scented beads in the bag. Compare that with the experience at the supermarket. You chuck your garment in with the milk and the frozen pizza, pull it out of the bag when you get home and drop it on the kitchen floor with the toothpaste and yoghurt. How do you feel about that garment when you put it on?

I have to tell you, it is highly unlikely that anyone will be successful if they don't have the passion for what they are doing, whether it is running a business, working at a job or studying to learn a skill. It has always helped me that I am doing what I enjoy. The one thing I wish is that I had more confidence. I target high-risk businesses so I come over as confident but, in reality, I'm just a person who does his homework.

On a personal note, I have really been helped by my family life. I have been married for thirty years and I've got five children from late twenties to not-yet-teens and a couple of grandchildren too. We married when I was eighteen, and it's been the bedrock of my life. Mrs P. rules the roost, and the minute my driver drops me off at home and I cross the threshold I am no longer the boss. No, the gloves are off. I get ordered about and have chores like everyone else and slot in as part of the team! Yes, having a stable family background is great. You have a nightmare day, and finally you say 'enough' and hurry back home. Of course, when you get there the kids are screaming at you and you want to go back to work. That's also a great motivator!

You are already on the first step to success, because you are reading and taking advice from other people. As a businessman, I can tell you it's very hard to find new talented people who are hungry for success, understand where they're going and who are willing to find and listen to expert advice. The secret is this: you don't have to be perfect, none of us are. But do listen to the people who have got more experience than you, whether it's a business contact or mentor. If someone says something sensible, take it on board and use it yourself. It's only common sense, right?

## 1. Get going!

Everybody's got to start somewhere. Take me. I was a kid from a north London comprehensive. I had problems with dyslexia and I couldn't read very well. So, how did I end up with millions? Answer: I jumped in and got going.

At fifteen, I was running the school tuck shop. I left school at sixteen and went into an insurance company. As the boss? No, as a tea-boy, assistant tea-boy even! But it got me used to the world of work.

Seriously, the best way to learn something is through actually doing it yourself, dealing with the stress, and finding out first-hand. So, don't hang around, get going! Do some training first, if it will really help. Then get a job, or start a business.

## 2. Be prepared

It always amazes me how many people turn up on *Dragons' Den* without ticking even the basic boxes. Everyone knows they will have to answer questions about their business. They're supposed to know it inside out because they live it every day. But viewers are always asking me, 'What was that idiot doing on your show without even knowing how to run their numbers?'

I'm here to tell you this doesn't just happen in the Den. It happens in business all the time. The answer is obvious. Like the boy scouts say, 'Be prepared'. Do your homework and nothing will come up that you won't be able to answer with style.

Whether you are going to an interview for your first job or taking over your twentieth business, being prepared makes a massive difference. Say some kid arrives on *Dragons' Den*. He may only be nineteen but he's got a great idea. What's more, he knows all the facts and figures, has checked out how to get the idea made, even sorted out complex legal stuff like patents and trademarks. Will I invest in him? You bet.

I owe my own success to preparation. Before I stand up in front of anyone I have the answers to any questions that they might ask me. I plan everything first and get it crystal clear in my mind. I say to myself, 'What if they say to me . . .?' and, 'What if they want to know about . . .?' I call this buttoning down the 'what-ifs'. Sure as anything, they will come up. Sort out what you are going to say in advance and you're much more likely to convince people to be on your side.

Get to know the other person's business too. Use a computer, find out about the people you're meeting and their company. Get the information you need to stay on top. The fact that other fools haven't got their ducks in a row is good, because it gives the rest of us a chance!

## 3. Common sense is not common

K.I.S.S. stands for 'Keep It Simple, Stupid'. When you've got a problem, take some time to sort it out and look for the common sense solution. In my view, ninety per cent of all business is about common sense. But amazingly, common sense is not common. If it was common, everyone would have it and everyone would be able to do what I do. Then how would I make a living?

Keep what you say simple too. Then people are more likely to buy into what you're trying to achieve. And, whatever you say, say it nicely. When I owned Millwall Football Club, I was recognised often because I did a lot of stuff on TV about football. Nowadays people want to talk to me about the *Den,* and most of them have got an idea they are bursting to try out. So I talk to them, keep it light-hearted, and tell them what I think in return. I always find that, as long as you are pleasant, people are decent and polite—and that way good things tend to happen.

## 4. Stay confident
You have to believe in yourself. If things go wrong, you've got to pick yourself up and try again. It's a lot better than not having a go in the first place.

So, how do you get confidence and success? That's hard to answer. Drive, ambition, dreams, plus the will to make it happen: you need all those. But you also have to deal with your fears. That's one of the lessons you need to learn, whether you're on *Dragons' Den* or standing in front of a possible employer or a bank manager or a tutor at a college you want to go to.

The first time I was in the Den, I was nervous as a kitten. Everyone else had done lots of television. They had a history together. I was the outsider coming in. But I told myself it was no worse than when you go and plead with the bank manager in his swanky office! Either way, you have to say to yourself, 'OK, I'm nervous'. Then you just get on with it.

I met a man who had been in business since he was twelve. He started out running a schoolboys' gardening and window cleaning outfit. In his teens he was chucked out of college because the staff said he was making too much money selling kitchens to take his studies seriously.

Unfortunately, a little later he forgot the old saying that 'a lack of profit is a cancer, but a lack of cash-flow is a killer heart attack' and his business went bust. But he picked himself up, had the good sense to watch the finances the next time and he is now back at the top of his game. His new company has gone from his back bedroom to major growth. It was all a matter of staying confident despite setbacks.

## 5. Enjoy yourself

Last, but not least, remember that standing still is going backwards! You've got to keep ahead of the game and set yourself new targets each year. That way you stay fresh, gain experience, and move faster.

And don't be a misery. Make sure that you are doing what you enjoy. This will add to your strength and determination to get to where you need to go. My personal motto? I say there are three reasons to be in business. 1. To make money. 2. To have fun. 3. To make money.

I've managed, now it's over to you!

# Duncan Bannatyne

## The Serial Businessman

Duncan Bannatyne grew up in Clydebank and joined the navy as a teenager. He spent his twenties moving from one job to another, and his business career began with an ice-cream van that he bought for £450. He quickly bought more vans, but later sold the business and set up a chain of nursing homes.

He sold his nursing home business, Quality Care Homes, for £46 million in 1996, and his children's nursery chain, Just Learning, for £22 million. He has since moved into health clubs, hotels and house building.

Duncan has been given an OBE for services to business and charity and was recently made an honorary doctor of science by Glasgow Caledonian University. He was also made an honorary fellow of UNICEF for his services to charity in 2003. Duncan has also helped fund two orphanages in Romania and Colombia, working with the charity Scottish International Relief.

Duncan was awarded Master and Overall Entrepreneur of the Year in 2003, and was ranked ninth in a table of the UK's Top One Hundred Entrepreneurs by the business magazine, Management Today, in 2005. Duncan is a people person and his story of success shows the importance of knowing and trusting your team.

\*　　\*　　\*

The single most important factor in any company is the people who work for it. They are even more important than the product itself, because staff can hold the difference between success and failure in their hands. The success of any company depends on using human resources well and hiring the right people for the right positions.

I maintain that every person has it within themself to become successful at work, because my own success has been somewhat accidental. Almost all my businesses have had an element of chance, and it's only when I look back that I realise what a good opportunity each idea was.

I was in my late twenties when I returned to the mainland after living in the Channel Islands for a few years. I can quite honestly tell you that at that time I had absolutely nothing! No qualifications, no job, no home. Perhaps everyone needs a kick-start to their career and this was mine. Of course I had options. I could have lived on the street or found myself a job, but with no qualifications the job would probably have been something I hated for next to no money. Instead, I started my own company.

I was selling cars at auction when I

spied an ancient ice-cream van slowly trundling into the lot. Straightaway, I decided to begin selling ice cream. Within a short space of time and with a lot of graft, I had acquired a fleet of vans and had begun to make a healthy profit. When I started Duncan's Super Ices I had nothing. I had no business experience, no degree, no assets, no capital and no influential contacts. But I learned quickly.

Each day I studied the performance of my fleet. I would tally the stock on every van from the start to the end of the day, and work out the profit margin for each vehicle. My daily accounting gave good results. It showed me who were the best drivers on my fleet and also allowed me to understand some problems. I found that some of my best drivers were being held back by their families. Their wives did not want them out working past 9 p.m., which was when some of the best money could be made. Even at this early stage of my business, I was learning to understand what type of person I should be looking for to fill certain jobs in my companies. I also learned to consider things such as family life and how that might affect a person's work.

I also learnt to be practical. I recall one occasion when I had two people working one of the ice-cream vans. They always made a decent profit for me, but I worked out that they were stealing £50 from the till each week. I talked to them about that and they ended up leaving. However, their replacement turned out to be a poor worker who stole even more money than they had, and so this once very profitable van began to make a loss. I realised that I must look at the bigger picture. Even though what the previous employees were doing was wrong, I was making a fair amount of money from their work and that was better than the van making a loss.

Some people enjoy the security of being hands-on all the time with their companies, but that goes against my belief that delegation is one of the keys to success. Even in those early days with the ice-cream vans, I knew that I was going to have to delegate because it wasn't physically possible for me to operate more than one van at once. Also, as soon as the time was right, I made sure I gave myself Saturdays off!

After I sold the ice-cream business, I set up Quality Care Homes for the elderly and began to expand and practise the ideas I had put in place with Duncan's Super Ices. I found that many of the nurses were incredibly hard-working and enthusiastic. They were passionate about ensuring that the residents were constantly active and always involved in activities and events. I wanted to give these outstanding employees the opportunity to develop their careers and their skills, and to reward them with promotion and greater responsibility. I watched how these people reacted to the changes and, if they grew with the job and handled the added pressure, I would reward them further. I found that it was all about variety. Different kinds of people were able to thrive in my companies and, in turn, help me to make my business a success. Of course, some people failed to take the chance that I gave them, but this did not stop me from encouraging my brightest staff.

It was because of a skiing accident that I set up Bannatyne's Health Clubs. My injured leg needed exercise, but my nearest gym was a twenty-five minute drive away. I decided to build a health club of my own for the people in my area. We now have more than sixty clubs throughout the UK.

Then I set up Just Learning, a chain of day-care centres for children, because I needed a nursery for my kids but all the centres had waiting lists. Clearly there was a demand that needed to be met. So I built my own.

Within five years we had more than twenty centres, which was a huge growth, and I sold the company for £22 million. These businesses, along with the care homes, were all quite different and aimed at different age groups. They all offered a valuable service to the local community, however, and I was able to re-use my basic ideas about staff in each of these companies.

Often, when a business is getting bigger, finding the right sort of staff becomes more difficult. As Bannatyne's Health Clubs got bigger, it quickly became clear that top-class managers and gym instructors were in demand, especially with a growing number of other branded health clubs around. This started to happen at our Just Learning centres too, and qualified staff became more and more difficult to find.

One way of getting the best staff would have been to offer higher wages than other companies. Yet I always search for people who believe in what we are trying to achieve, not people who are just joining for a few extra pounds in their wage packet. Therefore we introduced training within our companies. At Just Learning we encouraged employees to gain their National Vocational Qualifications (NVQs) while working with us. At Bannatyne's Health Clubs we encourage all our staff at every level to get training that can lead to promotion, greater responsibility and, of course, a better wage.

Rewarding honest, hard-working and talented staff helps to maintain the level of good service which is vital to children and their parents at the day-care centres and is always welcomed by gym members. It also goes a long way to make sure that morale is kept high and standards are maintained. I know I have reliable staff and, another important thing, the company saves money on hiring new people.

At the highest level of my work, I prefer to take an even more active role in finding and keeping people. All the people on my board of directors have come through the ranks of the business and have been working with me for a very long time. They enjoy their jobs, and I know that I can trust them to continue doing what I want them to do. I believe it works because I know who these people are. I do not need to play golf with staff to get to know them better, because I understand them through working with them and listening to them.

Because of this approach, a lot of people feel fulfilled by their management jobs. The key is to find these people and make them happy and content. Rewards are very important, and a few people who have worked with me have become millionaires through share options. Share options allow people to make a lot of money and to feel the benefit of their own work and talent.

With my health clubs, there are always targets for the staff to hit and generous bonuses on offer. Everybody benefits from the efforts of everybody else. The training at the day care centres brings out the best in my staff and allows them to take on more responsibility. For that they will be rewarded. Training at all stages of a career is important. Well-trained people move forward. That brings more money, more responsibility and more satisfaction for the employees. In turn, comes more growth, success and profit for the company as a whole.

I think I have some good instincts when it comes to hiring staff but, most of the time, my knowledge of someone will grow as I work with them. The instincts I have gained over the years come from knowing, living with, meeting, and working with a large number of people. I've met people who have literally lived in sewers, and I've sat on a board with high-powered, highly educated people. This range of experience has allowed me to develop a sense of the sort of people I enjoy working with. I do not always look for qualifications or lots of experience. I study the personality and, perhaps above all, I value loyalty. By delegating to trustworthy employees I am able to take a step back from the frenzy of the day-to-day business and examine the accounts, the bottom line which shows the profit. The art of delegation allows me much more time to enjoy the most important part of my life, my family, and to take plenty of relaxing holidays in the sun!

You can start your business career with something small, something that perhaps doesn't look likely to make you your fortune, but with hard work, common sense and a will to learn, anything is within your grasp. Look at me. I started with one ice-cream van! Who would have guessed that it would lead to chains of fitness centres, hotels, retirement homes and dance schools?

Here are some of the things I believe are most important for success in business and in life:

## 1. The people you choose to work for you

The people you work with are very important to the success of your company. After all, you could be selling the best gadget in the world or the most exciting service this side of Los Angeles, but if your people are not happy or not motivated or are simply lazy, your business will fail. It is not easy to choose who to give a job to, but I always look for enthusiastic people who are determined to succeed. To me, that is far more important than how many A-Levels they have.

Leadership is very much part of this. A successful company has people working for it who believe in what they are doing. This is easier in some areas than others, of course! But, even in the most boring business, there are lots of ways for you to encourage staff and help them to help the company. Ever since my days with the ice-cream business, I have made sure that I provide things like proper training, bonuses, and the chance for promotion to the staff who deserve it. The advantage is that I have known them for years. My staff are loyal and I prize that very highly.

## 2. Choosing the right product or service

I said above that the people working in your business can make or break you, however good your product is. A similar thing is true here. Even the very best people in the world will not be able to make a success of a business that is offering something that no one wants! On *Dragons' Den* I have seen many ideas that I know will not work because no one will buy them. Many people remember the inventor who

72

tried to sell us the cardboard beach chair. I still can't believe he didn't ever think of what might happen to the seat once someone dripping with sea water sat on it!

So you must be as sure as you can be that there is a demand for whatever you want to sell. You might have an idea totally by accident, but you still need to research it carefully. On *Dragons' Den* I am always interested in people who can prove that people want their product or service. So do your research before jumping in!

## 3. Organising your company and how it will work

All good companies need to be well organised. It sounds obvious, but organisation is something that many people do not pay enough attention to. Perhaps it's seen as boring and so some people ignore it, but it is very important. When I invest in a new company on *Dragons' Den,* I like to go in and solve some of their organisational problems. Sometimes the solutions are very simple.

First of all, you must understand how your company works. Who makes which decisions? Which people do what jobs? What is the most efficient way of doing things? Part of this is making sure, as a boss, that you can delegate. As a company grows you must accept that you cannot make every single decision yourself! That is why people and trust are so important. Being able to delegate means that I can stand back and take an overview of the whole business. I can make calm, rational improvements that I might not have seen otherwise. If you are an employee, you should try to understand how your company works so that you can work efficiently and get promoted.

### 4. Suppliers are important
It doesn't matter what business you are in, whether you own an airline or run a market stall, you need suppliers,

so make sure they are good ones! If you are not satisfied with their service, look elsewhere. If the suppliers are not helping you, this will affect your customers too and, if they become unhappy, your business will suffer. Getting the best suppliers needs research and probably some trial and error as well, but this will be worth it in the long run.

## 5. Communication is key to success

Like organisation, communication is something that can easily be forgotten. But you must not forget about it! All good companies need information and good communication. People need to understand what they are doing and why they are doing it. They need to be made aware easily and simply of any important changes. It's very basic really, but sometimes it's the basics that are ignored and that's when things go wrong. You can decide yourself how to make sure everyone communicates well with each other, whether by email or with regular meetings. But the key is always to make sure that no one is left in the dark.

## 6. Experience

Of course, you may start out like me with no experience in business at all. It's funny—some entrepreneurs spend their childhood selling homemade lemonade or washing cars, and going into business is natural to them. But that's not everyone. And not all of those eight-year-old business people turned into Richard Branson! What I think is important is to learn from your experience and from that of others. I had already set up several big companies by the time I started on *Dragons' Den*, but I have learned so much since being on the programme. For example, my knowledge is of service industries, so I have learned very interesting new things from Theo Paphitis, who is an expert in retail.

Always have your eyes and ears open and when you spot something new to you that seems to be working somewhere else, see how it might be able to help your own company.

All of these things are linked together. You need good people, but for them to work best they need a good product and they need to be keen to work for the company. Their enthusiasm can be affected by many things, but every company needs good organisation and communication to be able to work as smoothly as possible. If you can bring these things together, you have a great chance of success.

# James Caan

## The Investor

The newest recruit to Dragons' Den is James Caan. James sees Dragons' Den as a natural extension of his overall business plan, which has always been to find people who have a great business idea, a decent plan, and the drive and passion to succeed. Born in 1960, James Caan went into business at the age of twenty-four when he created the Alexander Mann Group (AMG). It quickly became one of the UK's top recruitment companies. James sold the company in two stages, having spent seventeen years developing it.

In 2002 James decided to take a year off and followed an Advanced Management Programme at Harvard University. Alexander Mann Group has continued to do well. Since its sale, James has invested in many businesses. In 2001 James won the Enterprise of the Year Award sponsored by BT, for outstanding success in business. In 2003 James was named Entrepreneur of the Year by PricewaterhouseCoopers, one of the UK's leading firms of accountants, and in the same year he won the entrepreneur category in the Asian Jewel Awards.

In 2005 he was included in the Asian Power One Hundred, the list of Britain's one hundred most influential and inspiring Asian people. James has spoken at Oxford University's Business School, and he has recently been a Resident Entrepreneur Mentor at the London Business School.

\*       \*       \*

I knew I was going to be a businessman from a very early age. My father ran a successful textile business and I naturally thought my career would be in business. However, having seen my father work seven days a week, eight hours a day, I realised that I needed to find something that interested and excited me but also allowed me to have a good quality of life.

I was never interested in school when I was young, and I didn't believe you needed an education in order to succeed. I left school in my teens and joined a small recruitment agency as a trainee interviewer. I earned £32 a week, plus £5 for every job I managed to fill. With telephone sales, you have to be able to cope with rejection and develop your own style, your own personality and confidence. I quickly got the hang of this and it soon became second nature to me.

I then went on to work for three recruitment agencies, each in a different industry. I did this to get experience of different businesses. One day, a client, a financial services company, was recruiting sales people.

The sales director was impressed with the way I'd understood their requirements. He took me out to lunch and offered me a job as recruitment manager of his company.

I met my wife, Aisha, at this company when she came for an interview. She had graduated from the London College of Fashion and was one of the lucky students to be taken on by a design house. After working there for a few months, she decided she wanted to set up her own business. Her father was keen for her to do so, and her dream was to run a shop called House of Aisha.

Aisha needed a job while she was setting up her company and that is when I interviewed her. I was attracted to her straightaway and so I asked her out. She told me about her business plans and I told her I wanted to back her. I went to a shopping centre in north London where Aisha had seen a vacant shop to let. We met the manager, who told Aisha that he was impressed and that she just needed to submit her plans to get a shop in the centre. I pretended to be overjoyed, and I congratulated Aisha, but secretly I was panicking. How was I going to find the money I had promised her?

Aisha needed £30,000. I couldn't ask my father for a loan because he'd tell me I was thinking with my heart, not with my head. I went to various banks but they all said 'no'. Then I realised that I could borrow a lot of money from different banks by using overdrafts. It was risky, but I got £30,000 of unsecured debt.

So we set Aisha up in the shop and it did really well. Of course, eventually, I had to tell her where the money came from, and she was horrified. She was shocked that I had promised to back her without actually having the money to do so. I apologised, but, at the same time, I explained that I had been confident in her drive to succeed, and that I would manage the money somehow. Where there's a will, there's a way. And I must have convinced her because, within a month of the shop opening, I asked her to marry me, and she accepted.

I was twenty-four when I started my first company, Alexander Mann. The name was my own invention. Indeed, I did everything myself. The idea behind Alexander Mann was to find staff for middle management jobs by headhunting. (Headhunting is recruiting staff by approaching people who are already working for one company and offering them a job at another company.) Until I started Alexander Mann headhunters only recruited top managers, directors who worked on company's boards, but I couldn't understand why middle managers shouldn't be recruited in this way. After all, they are the guys who make or break the company.

I picked up business very, very quickly, and it wasn't long before I was wondering whether this would work worldwide. I started a business called Humana International with my business partner Doug Bougie, and soon we had 147 offices in thirty countries.

Alexander Mann was a great success because I found a gap in the market, took a simple idea and then really promoted and developed it. Between 1985 and 1992, when I was building up the company, my understanding of how people worked and what made them tick grew hugely. Building a company is like watching a child grow. When I sold and handed over the keys to Alexander Mann Group, it was a very emotional moment for me. I'd started it from nothing, and at the time of handover it was turning over about £130 million a year in sales.

In 1992 I decided that I would start roughly one new business each year. The idea was actually similar to *Dragons' Den*. I would find somebody who had a good idea for a business and then I would put up the capital, develop the business and keep an eye on it for twelve months.

I've always enjoyed doing something creative with my money. Just piling up cash for the sake of it is not a great achievement. After all, it's what you do with the cash that makes you successful. I've never been a great saver. When I was young, if I was doing well, I'd want to buy a new suit or a car, or take a holiday. Spending the money would give me the drive to want to earn it all over again.

The best thing is to use cash to make things happen. Take my brothers and sisters, for instance. Rather than just buy gifts for my brothers and sisters, I've helped them to go into business for themselves. I've tried to understand what it is that each one of them can do and what they enjoy.

One weekend I went to the house of one of my sisters and she gave me some samosas. Now, I have grown up on samosas, but these were just amazing! So I suggested that she make some and sell them. 'What have you got to lose?' I asked her. So that Sunday she made 250 samosas, and by noon on Monday she had sold them all. Less than a month later she told me that she was making 1,000 and that they were sold as soon as they were ready. Seeing the potential, I put up the money for her to develop the business with a proper space and the right machinery. Now the business is called Nisa, and she makes 50,000 samosas a week. It just can't meet demand! It's great!

Another of my sisters trained as a beautician so I set her up in a beauty salon. One brother does alterations for Jaeger, Marks & Spencer, Hugo Boss and Calvin Klein. I encouraged my brother to run that business, which he now does very successfully. Another brother joined me running my recruitment business, and now he's set up his own business in Lahore supplying researchers for the recruitment business in the UK.

It's been a privilege to be a parent. My daughters are both at university, one studying politics and the other studying economics. They are two very bright girls who know their own minds. Being a parent has taught me a lot. You could say I have applied that knowledge to my business.

I learned that if I want my child to do something, I need to make her feel that it was her idea. For me, this same idea works in business. Both sides in a business agreement need to feel that they are gaining from the deal.

I think taking risks is a big part of being successful. He who dares, wins. You may think like me, or you may not. Everyone is different. But I do have several rules, or tips, that I believe can help people achieve the success they want:

## 1. Belief

You simply must have belief in yourself and in whatever it is you are selling or offering. You need to know that your product or service is good and that there is enough demand for it. My Alexander Mann business was a success because I knew I had found a gap in the market. If you do not have that belief, how can you expect anyone else to have it? For example, all my sister needed to start her samosa business was that bit of confidence, that belief, and she was away.

I believe that, if you have determination, if you're passionate, then you can make something work. Attitude is the key.

## 2. People, not product

I firmly believe it is people who produce success, not the product or the service itself. Whether I'm investing in a person or a business, in or out of *Dragons' Den*, it is the spirit and character of the person that is most important to me.

I value honesty and integrity in the people I work with above everything else. Success in business is about relationships and customers coming back for more. Customers will not return unless you prove they can trust you. You must also be able to trust the people you employ. After all your day-to-day business is in their hands. Honesty at work is very important. If you make a mistake, it's better to tell your employer so that it can be sorted out. An ability to communicate is important for entrepreneurs, too. If you wish to move on and start your own business, you will need to develop your leadership skills and being able to communicate clearly is vital.

Here's an example. A friend of mine came to me with an idea for a business of serviced offices. He would supply offices on long- or short-term contracts ready to use. These offices would be supplied with office equipment and cleaned—ready for a company to move in straightaway. On paper, there were dozens of reasons why I should have told him that I wasn't interested. But his character, his honesty and his belief convinced me to invest in his plan. Within just three years his passion had helped drive us on to owning ten centres in central London, and we sold the business for £25 million. This makes my point perfectly—this was a sector of business that was failing, but the people behind it forced it to succeed.

### 3. Be original

If you want to be successful, then you must be prepared to think differently to everyone else. Look at what you see around you—and if you are doing the same thing as everyone else, then think about making some changes. It can be hard to swim against the tide, but I believe that an ability to be different, to be individual, will help you a lot. As an entrepreneur, you need to be offering something a little bit different so as to stand out in a crowded market. Or, best of all, you might spot a gap in the market that no one else has thought of.

If you work for someone else, different ideas can sometimes be very useful. It might be that a simple idea can save or make your company money. This can only help your career!

## 4. Presentation

This one is common sense really and, dull as it may seem, presentation does matter. Whether you are applying for a job or to go on a course, working as part of a team or leading a group, presentation of yourself makes a difference. The clothes you wear say a lot about you, so think carefully.

Even if you don't think wearing a pair of old jeans will affect your work, others might, whether they are potential customers or those in a position to promote you or offer you a job. If you cannot make the best of yourself, they may think, how can they trust you to do your best for the business?

## 5. Clear calm communication

This is something so easy to get right, such a simple piece of advice, but it's well worth thinking about. You need to make sure that you can get your ideas across clearly and answer questions calmly. Confidence in yourself inspires people to have confidence in you.

## 6. Learn from failure

It's Del Boy's favourite saying, but that doesn't mean it's not true. Who dares, wins! But, of course, the world is littered with stories of great business people who have failed at one time or another. Many people have lost a job over the course of their careers. And many more people have messed up a job interview. It happens. But you need to learn from the experience and try again.

I once made a very quick decision to buy a large chain of sandwich shops. It looked like a fantastic investment. It was failing, but it was established and we felt we could turn it around and achieve some success. But I had rushed into it and, once we had invested, it became clear that the competition was too fierce and the product was not good enough. It was not an enjoyable experience, but I learned so much from examining why it failed—and, of course, I try not to repeat those same mistakes.

The lesson is that, whatever work you are involved in, you will always make mistakes. Everyone does. Try to plan for things not working out as you hope they will and, when you do experience a failure (and you will!), learn from it and bounce back. Don't get disheartened.

If you make a mistake at work, tell your employers and show them that you are ready to learn from that mistake. The plans that didn't work out are always the ones that stay in my head, that make me take extra care on the next deal or with my next decision. Sometimes, the experience of failure is more valuable than the experience of success.

## 7. Sacrifice

I think sacrifice is a very important trait. If you are trying to achieve success but you are not prepared to really put yourself out, then for me that's not enough. If I see someone who is willing to work long hours, perhaps someone who might even be willing to re-mortgage their own house for their business, then I know that what I have is someone who is more than just talk. It may be harsh, but there is no substitute for genuine hard work.

Looking over my tips, I suppose my real advice, or my message, is that it is all about YOU. No one can do the work for you, or provide passion for you, or achieve success for you. You have to do it yourself. It's your approach, your enthusiasm, your belief, that will help you to become a success. Forget what qualifications you have or don't have. Forget what you think you can or can't do. It is your attitude that will help you reach the heights!